SHOCKWAVE
SOCIAL STUDIES

Carved in Stone

CLUES ABOUT CULTURES

Yvonne Morrison

children's press®

An imprint of Scholastic Inc.

NEW YORK • TORONTO • LONDON • AUCKLAND • SYDNEY
MEXICO CITY • NEW DELHI • HONG KONG
DANBURY, CONNECTICUT

Library of Congress Cataloging-in-Publication Data

Morrison, Yvonne.
  Carved in stone : clues about cultures / by Yvonne Morrison.
      p. cm. -- (Shockwave)
  Includes index.
  ISBN-10: 0-531-17785-8 (lib. bdg.)
  ISBN-13: 978-0-531-17785-3 (lib. bdg.)
  ISBN-10: 0-531-15462-9 (pbk.)
  ISBN-13: 978-0-531-15462-5 (pbk.)
 1. Archaeology and history--Juvenile literature.
 2. Stone carving--Juvenile literature. 3. Antiquities--Juvenile literature.
 I. Title. II. Series.

   CC77.H5M65 2007
   930.1--dc22

2007022406

Published in 2008 by Children's Press, an imprint of Scholastic Inc.,
557 Broadway, New York, New York 10012
www.scholastic.com

08 09 10 11 12 13 14 15 16 17
10 9 8 7 6 5 4 3 2 1

Printed in China through Colorcraft Ltd., Hong Kong

Author: Yvonne Morrison
Educational Consultant: Ian Morrison
Editor: Frances Chan
Designer: Emma Alsweiler
Photo Researchers: Jamshed Mistry and Frances Chan

Photographs by: Big Stock Photo (pp. 3–6; Viking runes, Egyptian statues, Aboriginal rock
paintings, p. 7; Emperor's Army, p. 17; Hindu temple, p. 19; Lion of Lucerne, p. 21; Uxmal,
Mexico, p. 24; Native American petroglyphs, p. 26); **Getty Images** (cover; Algerian cave art,
pp. 8–9; Viking rune-stone, p. 20; Holocaust memorial, pp. 28–29); **Jennifer and Brian Lupton**
(teenagers, pp. 30–31); **Jens-Uwe Korff/www.creativespirits.de** (Burrup rock art, p. 11); © **LMR
Group/Alamy** (Easter Island statues, pp. 26–27); **Photolibrary** (amphora, stone coffins, stone
columns, pp. 14–15); **Stock.Xchng: Stéphane Vandenwyngaert** (Ramses II, p. 23); (Angkor Wat,
p. 7; Mount Rushmore pp. 16–17; Celtic cross, p. 25; Petra, pp. 30–31; **Tranz: Corbis** (p. 1; bison
painting, p. 9; Aboriginal woman, petroglyphs, pp. 10–11; pp. 12–13; Roman stone couch,
p. 15; Mamallapuram, pp. 16–17; Amiens Cathedral, Buddhist temple, pp. 18–19; Ethiopian tombs,
Mexican graveyard, pp. 20–21; Tower of London graffiti, Viking rune marks, pp. 22–23; gargoyles,
Chinese jade pendant, pp. 24–25, p. 27, World Trade Center Memorial, p. 28)

All illustrations and other photographs © Weldon Owen Education Inc.

CONTENTS

archaeologist (*ar kee OL uh jist*) a scientist who studies people and objects of the past

hieroglyph (*hy roh GLIFF*) a picture or symbol that stands for a sound, a word, or an idea

memorial (*muh MOR ee uhl*) something that is built or done to help people continue to remember a person or an event

monument (*MON yuh muhnt*) a statue or building that is built to remind people of a person or an event

obelisk (*AHB uh lisk*) an upright stone pillar with a top shaped like a pyramid

petroglyph (*PET roh gliff*) a drawing or carving made on rock

prehistoric dating from a time before historical events were written down

For easy reference, see Wordmark on back flap.
For additional vocabulary, see Glossary on page 32.

Glyph is from the Greek language, and means "to hollow out, engrave, or carve." The prefix added to *glyph* defines the type of carving – *hiero* refers to picture, or sacred; *petro* refers to rock.

The study of ancient people is fascinating. How did they live? What did they do all day? Did they think the same way as we do? These questions and many more can be answered by studying the clues ancient people left behind. Since early humans picked up pieces of charcoal and scratched pictures on cave walls, people have been recording the world around them. In some cases, they wrote on paper or cloth, which has broken down over time and is now lost forever. But when people carved in stone, they were making records that would last indefinitely. Ancient people have left stone carvings on every continent of the world, except Antarctica.

Native Americans in the U.S. carved pictures onto rocks.

The Inca of Peru built walls of perfectly matched stones.

North America

South America

The Vikings of Sweden, Norway, and Denmark left **rune** symbols carved in stone.

Carvings and statues are seen all over temples in Egypt.

The temple at Angkor Wat in Cambodia is covered with carvings.

Europe

Asia

Africa

Australia

Antarctica

Aboriginal rock paintings are found in many parts of Australia.

VOICES OF THE PAST

The hunting has been good today. Working together, the men have managed to bring down a large beast with their sharpened spears. They have brought it back to the cave. The women have skinned the beast and sliced it into chunks to be roasted on sticks. Now the people sit around the fire, happy because their bellies are full. One of the men gets up. He licks the grease off his fingers and picks up a sharp-edged stone. By the light of the flames, he begins to scratch a line into the cave wall.

Ten thousand years later, **archaeologists** explore the cave. They find the man's artwork. It is a picture of the hunt, showing a group of men throwing spears at a large creature with horns. It is by no means a **sophisticated** drawing. But it shows the archaeologists how the ancient people hunted and which animals they killed. The story of that successful hunt lives on.

In the past, events or stories were often recorded in stone. Some pictures were carved, or etched. Some were drawings or paintings on stone. Most stone lasts forever. It is a permanent record. By studying stone carvings, we can learn how ancient people lived. We can discover what was important to them.

These cave paintings were made about 10,000 years ago in Algeria, North Africa.

In 1992, a youth group in France scrubbed off some **prehistoric** cave paintings by mistake! The youths were doing a cleanup project. Officials wanted to charge the group with **vandalism**. But the group said that there were no signs to show that the area was protected.

Cool Caves

Some of the best-known prehistoric cave paintings can be found in Lascaux (*Lah SCOH*), France. The art dates back to somewhere between 15,000 and 13,000 B.C. There are nearly 2,000 painted figures. They are mainly of horses, stags, bison, and bulls. There's only one picture of a human.

The caves were discovered in 1940 by four teenagers. After that, there were so many visitors to the caves that the atmosphere inside the caves was affected. The paintings began disintegrating. The caves were closed in 1963 so that the paintings could be restored. In 1983, Lascaux II was opened. This is a **replica** of two of the cave halls, located a short walk from the original cave.

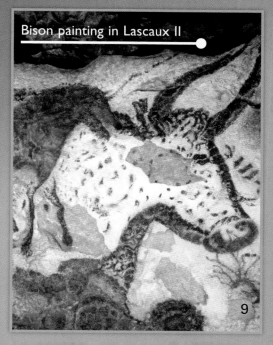

Bison painting in Lascaux II

I think the author used italics in the first paragraph to make sure the reader understands that this part is a dramatization. This is an interesting way of introducing the topic. It sure got my attention!

9

THE ART OF DREAMING

Aboriginal **petroglyphs**, Australia

Ancient people must have had a strong desire to produce artwork. They could not buy tools and paints at the local store, as we can. All of their materials would have been made by hand. This is a lot of trouble to go to. Why did they bother? Weren't they too busy with survival activities, such as hunting and making shelters? No! The evidence shows that creating pictures was an important part of their lives too.

Rock art by the **Aborigines** of Australia dates back 40,000 years. That makes the art in Australia about eight times older than the Egyptian pyramids, which were built almost 5,000 years ago.

In Western Australia, thousands of ancient Aboriginal petroglyphs are under threat. **Acid rain** from chemical factories in Burrup Peninsula has already destroyed many carvings. Now the Western Australian government has approved plans to build a gas-processing plant. This will add to the pollution. The World **Monuments** Fund has listed Burrup as one of the top 100 most **endangered** heritage sites on the planet. It seems that no protected area is safe from industrial progress!

Ancient artists:
- couldn't buy tools or paints at stores
- had to use handmade tools and materials
- were very busy just surviving

Aboriginal petroglyphs, Australia

Burrup rock carving of a figure

The petroglyphs depict extinct animals, marine animals, such as saltwater crocodiles, and freshwater animals, such as geese and platypuses (*PLAT uh pussiz*).

Many Aboriginal paintings also show images of the Dreaming, or Dreamtime. The Dreaming explains the origins of the land and the Aboriginal people. The drawings are usually in red **ocher**. They show stick-like human figures in fighting, hunting, and dancing scenes. Some paintings of the Dreaming are said to be by spiritual beings rather than humans.

Did You Know?

The earliest people made sculpting tools from stone and bone. The hardest stone in Europe and Africa was flint. In Asia, people used quartzite and fossilized wood. Metal tools came into use around 4000 B.C. The Egyptians were among the first people to make copper tools. Later, bronze and iron tools helped in the development of the art of sculpture.

ONCE UPON A TIME

Today, stories of both true and fictional events are told in newspapers, history books, and on the Internet. These stories are written in words and often accompanied by photographs.

Egyptian hieroglyphs

By contrast, stories from long ago are largely told through the artwork that ancient people left behind. Sometimes the artwork is just carved pictures. Sometimes it is words. Sometimes it is picture-words, known as **hieroglyphs**. The ancient Mayans used square-shaped hieroglyphs as a form of writing. Large, sandstone pillars covered with hieroglyphs have been found at Mayan ruins. They recount important historical events, such as battles.

Perhaps the best-known hieroglyphs are those of ancient Egypt. The Israel Stela is a ten-foot-tall stone block carved with hieroglyphs. It was discovered in 1896 in the **tomb** of King Merenptah. It is now in the Egyptian Museum in Cairo. The hieroglyphic text has been translated. The text describes in a very poetic way the king's amazing abilities. It lists all the king's victories, telling that he dealt bravely with his enemies and caused terror in their hearts. Reading Egyptian hieroglyphs is one of the best ways for historians to work out the history of ancient Egypt.

Mayan hieroglyphs

Mini Stories

Not all carvings were done to record historical events. Native American sculptors from the southwestern United States carved small stone figures of animals, humans, and spirits to help them remember fictional stories. The little carvings are called storytellers or fetishes. The **Navajo** string the fetishes together to make story necklaces.

Did You Know?

When somebody says their plans are "set in stone," this does not mean that they have used a chisel to carve their plans into the side of a cliff! The person just means that the plans are final. The saying comes from the fact that words and images set down in stone last a long time. They are not easily changed.

UNCOVERING HISTORY

Some ancient stone carvings, such as those on the temples in Egypt, are easy to spot. Others are hidden in caves. Some ancient **artifacts** are completely buried under the floor of the ocean. Uncovering these objects is the work of marine archaeologists. They spend their days diving deep under the ocean, hoping to recover long-lost treasures. It is often hard to spot artifacts. They are usually covered with thick layers of **barnacles**, making them look like part of the ocean floor. Fish and other marine life are distracting too!

Roman shipwrecks have been found all over the Mediterranean Sea. Most of the ships carried amphorae – jugs that were used for storing liquids, such as wine or oil. Archaeologists have also discovered larger items, such as stone coffins, stone furniture, and even huge Roman columns.

When a shipwreck is being excavated, artifacts are taken from the site and catalogued. Some are exhibited in museums. Others are sold. Some archaeologists want shipwrecks to be left untouched so that people can explore them. All shipwrecks found in French waters are fully protected by the French government. However, this has not prevented scuba-diving thieves from stealing artifacts from the sites.

Amphora found off the coast of Israel

Stone coffins found off the coast of Greece

Sculptures Under the Sea

In Baia Bay near Naples, Italy, you can see an underwater town! Baia was once a vacation spot for wealthy ancient Romans. Thousands of years ago, parts of Baia were submerged by volcanic activity. Today, the bay is the site of a protected underwater archaeological park. You can view it from a glass-bottomed boat or explore it by scuba diving. There are remains of roads, house walls, tiled floors, columns, and spa baths.

Roman stone couch found at Baia

Stone columns found off the coast of Israel

LIFESTYLES OF THE RICH AND FAMOUS

Throughout history, societies have celebrated important people by having their likenesses carved in stone. More than 1,000 years ago, huge sandstone cliffs at Mamallapuram in South India were carved with the images of kings and queens. The images stand alongside gods and goddesses – a way of emphasizing the importance of royalty. Mamallapuram also features cave temples and gigantic open-air **reliefs** carved in granite dating back to the seventh century.

> **?** The opening sentence is very helpful in setting the scene. I could be pretty sure this page would feature carvings of famous people. It helps to be able to predict what will be on a page.

Statues of powerful leaders and inspiring public figures can be found in all the countries of Europe. Many of these were carved in marble or limestone. These stones were quarried extensively in Italy and France. The styles in which the statues were made, such as **Gothic** or **Renaissance**, reflect their period in history.

Mount Rushmore is a massive monument in America. This granite mountain has the heads of four U.S. presidents carved into it. Two million people visit it each year. They are awestruck by the monument's proportions. It covers 1,278 acres and is 5,725 feet above sea level.

The Emperor's Army

In 247 B.C., as soon as he became emperor, Qin Shi Huangdi (*Chin Shihr HWAHNG dee*) of China had thousands of workers begin making his tomb. He was only thirteen years old. The tomb took 36 years to finish. It was well hidden. Then, in 1974, a group of local people digging a well discovered Qin's tomb. Inside were 8,000 life-sized **terra-cotta** figures of warriors and horses. They were arranged in battle formation. Each of the statues is unique.

Mamallapuram, India

Mount Rushmore, South Dakota

SHOCKER

There are rumors that Qin had his workers buried alive to keep the location of the tomb secret. Human remains have been found near the terra-cotta army.

PLEASING THE GODS

Cultures from around the world create works of art to pay tribute to a higher being. Some cultures do this by carving images of that being and making offerings. By using the strongest materials available to them, people hope that their stone carvings will please their gods. In return, they hope that their gods will protect them. The ancient Greeks believed in a group of gods and goddesses who lived high on a mountain and controlled the lives of humans. In order to appeal to their gods and goddesses, the Greeks built temples. They decorated them with reliefs and sculptures carved from marble.

Hindu temples found throughout Asia are intricately carved. In some temples, almost every surface is covered with images of Hindu gods and characters from mythology. **Buddhist** temples feature carvings of Buddha. Buddha was a man who lived long ago and who was respected for having **compassion** for every living thing.

Many **Christian** churches contain carvings of religious figures, including angels and saints. The enormous Gothic cathedral in Amiens (*A MYENH*), France, has sculptures of saints standing shoulder to shoulder over its arched entranceway. These days, the statues are white, but paint chips show that they were once brightly painted.

Amiens Cathedral, France

Carving for Buddha

The world's biggest Buddhist temple is Borobudur (*Boar uh ba DOOR*) in Indonesia. This temple is the largest ancient monument in the southern hemisphere. It has 1,460 carved reliefs that show the teachings of Buddha. In total, there are 504 statues of Buddha!

SHOCKER

Some ancient cultures used stone **altars** for **sacrifices**. Grooves were carved into the stone to allow the victim's blood to flow away.

Ancient Greek temples
• carvings of gods and goddesses

Hindu temples
• Hindu gods, mythological characters

Buddhist temples
• carvings of the man, Buddha

Christian churches
• religious figures, angels, and saints

Hindu temple covered with carvings, India

19

REST IN PEACE

If you have ever visited a graveyard, you will have seen **memorials** carved in a stone such as granite or marble. Often the family has had a poem or favorite saying carved into the headstone to make it more personal. In Mexico, tombs are decorated to reflect the personality of the dead person. They are brightly colored and adorned with pictures.

In ancient Sweden and Norway, Vikings marked grave sites with rune-stones. The special rune symbols were meant to ease the dead person's passage into the next world. They also sometimes documented how much land the deceased owned and which relatives would inherit it. From about 300 A.D. to 500 A.D. in Ethiopia, important people had **obelisks** placed on their tombs. These massive stone pillars were carved to look like tall buildings, with windows, doors, and locks! In medieval England, important people, such as knights, had life-sized sculptures of themselves placed on top of their tombs, as if they were sleeping.

Sometimes large groups of people die over a short period of time, as in a war or natural disaster. When tragedies like this happen, communities often get together to build a large, long-lasting memorial.

Gravestones in Mexico

Viking rune-stone

Dying Lion

One of the most impressive memorials is the "Lion of Lucerne," in Switzerland. This sad statue of a dying lion was carved directly into the side of a sandstone cliff. It honors the loyal Swiss guards who died in 1792 during the French Revolution. More than 700 guards were killed while protecting the palace of King Louis XVI. Unfortunately, they were unaware that the king was no longer inside.

Tombs in Ethiopia, about 300 A.D.

Did You Know?

In medieval England, some tombstones featured carvings of animals to represent that person's character. A figure of a dog showed that the person had been faithful. A lion showed that the person had been courageous.

21

GRAFFITI IN STONE

Graffiti is the name given to marks made by people illegally in public places. In most countries, graffiti is considered a form of vandalism and is against the law. You may think graffiti is a modern thing, but it isn't! For thousands of years, people have wanted to leave their names behind them. Roman soldiers carved notes in caves. They wrote about their friends. They even insulted their enemies. One piece reads, "Samius to Cornelius: go hang yourself!"

The Tower of London, in England, has held many famous prisoners since it was built in 1066. Kings, queens, and political prisoners have been imprisoned there. Many of them carved graffiti into the tower's stone walls, leaving names, dates, and their final thoughts before being beheaded. Much of the graffiti remains today. One prisoner wrote, "Be faithful unto death."

As well as on grave sites, Viking rune symbols have been found in churches and on statues throughout Europe. Archaeologists thought that the runes carried important messages. But when translated, it was discovered that many of them said unremarkable things, such as "Olaf was here!"

Graffiti carved by prisoners, Tower of London, England

Ruining the Ruins

There is one famous graffiti artist who should have known better. Giovanni Belzoni was an ex-circus strongman from Italy. In the early 1900s, he discovered many ancient Egyptian ruins, including a statue of Ramses II (below). Instead of carefully preserving the ruins, Belzoni carved his name into many of them. Belzoni said that there was no better place to carve his name. These structures had lasted thousands of years, he reasoned, so they would most likely last for thousands more, carrying his name into the future!

Viking rune marks in a church in Turkey

The word *graffiti* comes from the Italian word *graffito*, meaning "a scratch or scribble." In ancient times, there were no fax machines or photocopiers. Graffiti was a legitimate way of getting your message across.

I Love What You've Done With the Place!

Sometimes ancient people made carvings in stone not because they wanted to leave a message, but because they wanted to make the place look nice. Just like today, people have always appreciated attractive surroundings. At Uxmal (*Oosh MAHL*), an ancient Mayan city in Mexico, most of the carvings on the buildings are complex shapes and patterns. These carvings are thought to have been purely for decoration.

Stone ornaments were often used to decorate buildings. Gargoyles are carved spouts that guide rainwater away from buildings. Most of these strange figures are found on medieval castles and churches. The ancient Greeks also made them, usually in the shape of a lion's head. A grotesque is another kind of fanciful carved creature on the outside of a building. Grotesques do not serve as waterspouts. Why decorate a building with fearsome creatures? Some people believe that gargoyles and grotesques are protectors that keep away evil.

The Celtic people of ancient Scotland decorated many objects with knot-work carvings. These look like a never-ending ribbon tied in a knotted design. They also used many spiral and key-shaped designs.

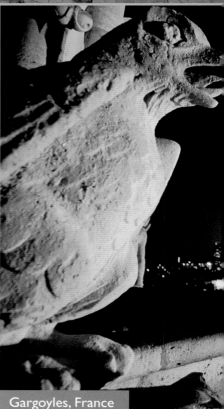
Gargoyles, France

Uxmal, Mexico

The Chain Bridge in Budapest, Hungary, is decorated with carved lions. Their mouths are slightly open, but the sculptor forgot to carve their tongues inside. Apparently, when he realized his mistake, the sculptor drowned himself in the river below!

Gargoyle comes from the French word *gargouille*, meaning "throat or waterspout." When water comes out of the gargoyle, it makes a gurgling sound. This is where we get the word *gargle* from.

Ancient Accessories

It was not just buildings that ancient people decorated with carvings. Hard stone and gemstones were worked into jewelry, such as rings, bracelets, and necklaces. Stone jewelry, such as the jade pendant below, was usually finely carved by hand. However, a 2,550-year-old jade ring found in China shows signs of having been made with complex machines!

Chinese jade pendant, made about 500 B.C.

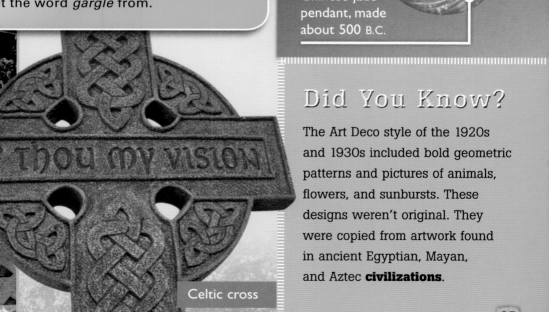

Celtic cross

Did You Know?

The Art Deco style of the 1920s and 1930s included bold geometric patterns and pictures of animals, flowers, and sunbursts. These designs weren't original. They were copied from artwork found in ancient Egyptian, Mayan, and Aztec **civilizations**.

Native American petroglyphs

For the most part, the carvings and artifacts left behind by ancient civilizations hold little meaning for people of today. It is archaeologists and historians who debate the original significance of these relics.

In some Native American petroglyphs, there are strange-shaped figures with circles and lines coming out of their heads. Archaeologists think these drawings show buffalo-horn headdresses and ear ornaments. The figures may be **shamans** or other important individuals. A figure with a whirlwind head may show a shaman's ability to fly as a supernatural being.

Easter Island statues

Easter Island (Rapanui) is a mysterious place in the South Pacific Ocean. Here you can see the remains of about 600 giant carved stone statues built between 900 A.D. and 1500 A.D. Most are 11 to 20 feet tall, but some are much taller. Archaeologists estimate that there were once another 250 statues, placed around the perimeter of the island. Were the statues erected to protect the island? Did they represent chiefs who once lived? Most likely they were symbols of religious and political power. It is certain, however, that it would have taken rollers, ramps, ropes, and huge amounts of human energy to move them into place.

Mysterious Stones

Stonehenge is a famous circle of stones in southwestern England. Archaeologists believe it was built in three main stages, from about 2800 B.C to 1500 B.C. The original monument had two circles of stones, with two horseshoes of stones inside. The tallest stones are more than 13 feet high.

The reason for the structure is still a mystery. Was it used for astronomy, religious ceremonies, or sacrifices? Did ordinary folk gather there or was it used only by important people? There were once 30 standing stones in the outside circle. Over the years, people have taken them to build bridges and dams. Scientists believe that it would have taken about 500 people to move one of the stones a short distance.

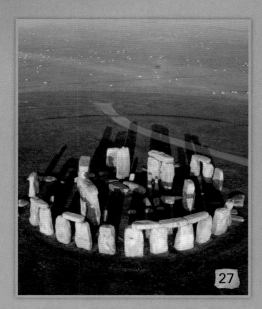

27

Future memorial for World Trade Center site, New York City

Thousand of years from now, archaeologists may study our culture. What will they learn from the art and **technology** that we have left behind? Most of our paper and digital records will not have survived. It will be plastic, metal, and stone objects that tell the most about our civilization.

Will future archaeologists understand the significance of today's memorials? The Holocaust Memorial in Berlin consists of 2,711 concrete slabs. The slabs represent the millions of Jewish people killed by the Nazis during World War II. A memorial is being planned for the site of the World Trade Center in New York City.

Holocaust Memorial, Berlin

It will honor all those who lost their lives in the terrorist attacks of September 11, 2001. The memorial will feature two large reflecting pools, representing the footprints of the towers that fell.

What will people of the future make of our artifacts? Will they think TV sets were once worshipped like gods? Will they think our garden tools were weapons of war? Will they think our refrigerators were treasure chests? It makes you wonder how accurate we are about objects from the past. Archaeologists must use all the clues they can to ensure their guesses are as close to the truth as possible.

Art for Aliens

In 1972 and 1973, two spacecraft, *Pioneer 10* and *Pioneer 11,* were launched into space. These probes contain special equipment to gather data about Jupiter. They also have a message for any aliens that might find them. Because scientists didn't know how to communicate with aliens, they attached a carved aluminum plaque to each probe. The plaques measure 9 inches by 6 inches. Using symbols, the plaques show the relative position of the sun in the galaxy, a diagram of the solar system, and the location of Earth. They also have figures of a man and a woman in front of a silhouette of a spacecraft. Both spacecraft left the solar system in the 1980s.

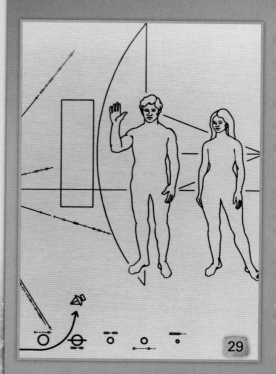

...New Seven Wonders of the World were announced in July 2007. All of them were carved in stone. They are Petra in Jordan, Machu Picchu in Peru, the Great Wall of China, Chichén Itzá in Mexico, the Colosseum in Rome, Italy, the statue of Christ the Redeemer in Brazil, and the Taj Mahal in India. Other finalists included the Giza pyramids in Egypt, Stonehenge in England, Angkor Wat in Cambodia, and the Easter Island statues.

WHAT DO YOU THINK?

Should ancient monuments be protected behind fences?

PRO

The Wonders of the World have lasted for thousands of years. It would be terrible if they were damaged now because of careless people. Even though a fence might be ugly, it's still better to have a fence than no ancient monuments!

Petra, Jordan

Millions of tourists flock to these sites every year. Unfortunately, their presence is slowly damaging these ancient artifacts. There is now a landslide risk at Machu Picchu. Parts of the trail may have to be closed. Stonehenge is now surrounded by a fence to protect it from damage. Some parts of Giza are now closed to the public. This is to stop people from climbing the monuments or writing graffiti inside the tombs.

CON

Putting an ugly fence around monuments spoils the view for people who come to see them. All ancient monuments need protecting, so maybe they should be guarded properly. That way, people can still see the monuments the way they were meant to be seen. They could also have a daily limit on the number of tourists allowed to visit.

Go to **www.new7wonders.com** to learn more about the New Seven Wonders of the World.

GLOSSARY

Aborigine (*ab uh RIJ uh nee*) one of the original or earliest known inhabitants of Australia

acid rain rain containing acids that form in the air because of pollution

altar a large table, used in religious ceremonies

artifact an object made by people from an earlier time

barnacle (*BAR nuh kuhl*) a small shellfish that attaches itself firmly to the sides of boats, rocks, and other objects in the ocean

Buddhist (*BOO dist*) a person who follows the teachings of Buddha

Christian (*KRISS chun*) a person who believes in the teachings of Jesus

civilization a highly developed and organized society

compassion a feeling of sympathy for, and a desire to help, someone who is suffering

endangered in danger of becoming extinct

Gothic a style of architecture used in western Europe between the twelfth and sixteenth centuries

Hindu (*HIN doo*) a person who believes in the religion of Hinduism, common in India

Navajo a group of Native Americans who live mainly in New Mexico, Arizona, and Utah

ocher (*OH ker*) a mineral found in earth that can be colored yellow, orange, red, or brown

relief figures or designs that are raised on a surface

Renaissance (*REN uh sahnts*) the period in European history that began in Italy in about 1300 and lasted until 1600

replica a copy or reproduction

rune something written in the characters of ancient alphabets

sacrifice an offering to a god or gods of something precious

shaman (*SHAY muhn*) a person who acts as medium between the natural and supernatural worlds, and who uses healing powers to cure illness

sophisticated (*suh FISS tuh kay tid*) cleverly designed or complex

technology the specific methods, materials, and devices used to solve practical problems

terra-cotta a brownish orange clay

tomb (*TOOM*) a small building where a dead person is buried

vandalism the needless damage or destruction of someone else's property

INDEX